The Poem of Hashish

By Charles Baudelaire &
Aleister Crowley

Copyright © 2020 Lamp of Trismegistus. All rights reserved. No part of this publication may be reproduced or transmitted in any form or by any means, electronic or mechanical, including photocopying, recording, or by any information storage and retrieval system, without permission in writing from Lamp of Trismegistus. Reviewers may quote brief passages.

ISBN: 978-1-63118-484-0

Esoteric Classics

Other Books in this Series and Related Titles

Confessions of an English Opium-Eater by T De Quincey (978-1-63118-485-7)

Qabbalistic Teachings and the Tree of Life by M P Hall (978-1-63118-482-6)

The Kabbalah of Masonry & Related Writings by E Levi &c (978-1-63118-453-6)

The Sepher Yetzirah and the Qabalah by M P Hall (978-1-63118-481-9)

Fortune-Telling with Dice by Astra Cielo (978-1-63118-466-6)

History, Analysis and Secret Tradition of the Tarot by Hall &c (978-1-63118-445-1)

Crystal Vision Through Crystal Gazing by Achad (978-1-63118-455-0)

Ancient Mysteries and Secret Societies by M P Hall (978-1-63118-410-9)

The Secrets of Enoch by Enoch (978-1-63118-449-9)

The Path of Light: A Manual of Maha-Yana Buddhism (978-1-63118-471-0)

The Rosicrucian Chemical Marriage by Christian Rosenkreuz (978-1-63118-458-1)

Ghosts in Solid Form by Gambier Bolton (978-1-63118-469-7)

American Indian Freemasonry by A C Parker (978-1-63118-460-4)

The Mysteries of Freemasonry & the Druids by M P Hall &c (978-1-63118-444-4)

Psalms of Solomon by King Solomon (978-1-63118-439-0)

Arcane Formulas or Mental Alchemy by W W Atkinson (978-1-63118-459-8)

The Machinery of the Mind by Dion Fortune (978-1-63118-451-2)

The Gospel of the Nativity of Mary by St. Matthew (978-1-63118-448-2)

Buddhist Psalms by Shinran (978-1-63118-465-9)

The Leadbeater Reader: A Selection of Occult Essays (978-1-63118-483-3)

The Human Aura: Astral Colors and Thought Forms (978-1-63118-419-2)

Audio versions are also available on Audible, Amazon and Apple

Table of Contents

Introduction...7

The Poem of Hashish

The Longing for Infinity...9

What is Hashish?...13

The Playground of the Seraphim...17

The Man-God...39

Moral...53

INTRODUCTION

The word "esoteric" can be difficult to define. Esotericism in general can be seen less as a system of beliefs and more as a category, which encompasses numerous, different systems of beliefs. It's a bit of juxtaposition, since the word "esoteric" indicates something that few people know about, while the term itself broadly covers numerous philosophies, practices, areas of study and belief systems.

In a greater sense, Esotericism acts as a storehouse for secret knowledge, which is often considered ancient (by *tradition, if not by fact),* passed down from generation to generation, in private. At various times in history, simply possessing the knowledge of some of these subjects, was considered illegal and a jailable offence, if discovered. This usually included such general topics as Alchemy, Pharmacology, Qabalah, Hermeticism, Occultism, Ceremonial Magic, Astrology, Divination, Rosicrucianism and so on. Collectively, these areas of study were often referred to as the esoteric sciences.

Sometimes, the outer garment of a subject isn't esoteric, while what is hidden beneath it, is. As an example, Freemasonry isn't necessarily esoteric by nature (at *least not anymore),* but certain signs, passwords and handshakes given to the candidate during their initiation, are in fact, esoteric, in the sense that they are hidden from the general public.

Today, in the twenty-first century, such topics are readily available at bookstores across the country, and numerous mainsteam publishers offer beginners guides and coffee-table volumes on many of these subjects, intended for mass appeal. Books like *"The Secret"* have turned previously arcane topics into household knowledge. All that being the case, however, it isn't to say that there still aren't buried secrets to uncover, ancient wisdom being ignored and forgotten mysteries to be explored. In fact, it is often that we are only able to further our own studies by standing on the shoulders of these disappearing giants.

Lamp of Trismegistus is doing its part to help preserve humanity's esoteric history by making some of these classics available to those students who are seeking to unearth the knowledge of these ancient colossi.

So, be sure to check other titles from our *Esoteric Classics* series, as well as our *Occult Fiction, Theosophical Classics, Foundations of Freemasonry Series, Supernatural Fiction, Paranormal Research Series, Studies in Buddhism* and our *Christian Apocrypha Series*. You can also download the audio versions of most of these titles from Amazon, Apple or Audible, for learning on the go.

CHAPTER I:
THE LONGING FOR INFINITY

Those who know how to observe themselves, and who preserve the memory of their impressions, those who, like Hoffmann, have known how to construct their spiritual barometer, have sometimes had to note in the observatory of their mind find seasons, happy days, delicious minutes. There are days when man awakes with a young and vigorous genius. Though his eyelids be scarcely released from the slumber which sealed them, the exterior world shows itself to him with a powerful relief, a clearness of contour, and a richness of colour which are admirable. The moral world opens out its vast perspective, full of new clarities.

A man gratified by this happiness, unfortunately rare and transient, feels himself at once more an artist and more a just man; to say all in a word, a nobler being. But the most singular thing in this exceptional condition of the spirit and of the senses -- which I may without exaggeration call heavenly, if I compare it with the heavy shadows of common and daily existence -- is that it has not been created by any visible or easily definable cause. Is it the result of good hygiene and of a wise regimen? Such is the first explanation which suggests itself; but we are obliged to recognise that often this marvel, this prodigy, so to say, produces itself as if it were the effect of a superior and invisible power, of a power exterior to man, after a period of the abuse of his physical faculties. Shall we say that it is the reward of assiduous prayer and spiritual ardour? It is certain that a constant elevation of the desire, a tension of the spiritual forces in a heavenly direction, would be the most proper regimen for creating this moral health, so brilliant and so glorious. But what absurd law causes it to manifest itself (as it sometimes does) after shameful orgies of the imagination; after a sophistical abuse of reason, which is, to its straightforward and rational use, that which the tricks of dislocation which some acrobats have taught themselves to perform are to sane gymnastics? For this reason I prefer to consider this abnormal condition of the spirit as a true grace; as a magic mirror wherein man is invited to see himself at his best; that is to say, as that which he should be, and might be; a kind of angelic excitement; a rehabilitation of the most flattering type. A certain Spiritualist School, largely represented in England and America, even considers supernatural phenomena, such as the apparition of phantoms, ghosts, &c, as manifestations of the Divine Will, ever anxious to awaken in the spirit of man the memory of invisible truths.

Besides this charming and singular state, where all the forces are balanced; where the imagination, though enormously powerful, does not drag after it into perilous adventures the moral sense; when an exquisite sensibility is no longer tortured by sick nerves, those councillors-in-ordinary of crime or despair; this marvellous state, I say, has no prodromal symptoms. It is as unexpected as a ghost. It is a species of obsession, but of intermittent obsession; from which we should be able to draw, if we were but wise, the certainty of a nobler existence, and the hope of attaining to it by the daily exercise of our will. This sharpness of thought, this enthusiasm of the senses and of the spirit, must in every age have appeared to man as the chiefest of blessings; and for this reason, considering nothing but the immediate pleasure he has, without worrying himself as to whether he were violating the laws of his constitution, he has sought, in physical science, in pharmacy, in the grossest liquors, in the subtlest perfumes, in every climate and in every age, the means of fleeing, were it but for some hours only, his habitaculum of mire, and, as the author of "Lazare" says, "to carry Paradise at the first assault." Alas! the vices of man, full of horror as one must suppose them, contain the proof, even though it were nothing but their infinite expansion, of his hunger for the Infinite; only, it is a taste which often loses its way. One might take a proverbial metaphor, "All roads lead to Rome," and apply it to the moral world: all roads lead to reward or punishment; two forms of eternity. The mind of man is glutted with passion: he has, if I may use another familiar phrase, passion to burn. But this unhappy soul, whose natural depravity is equal to its sudden aptitude, paradoxical enough, for charity and the most arduous virtues, is full of paradoxes which allow him to turn to other purposes the overflow of this overmastering passion. He never imagines that he is selling himself wholesale: he forgets, in his infatuation, that he is matched against a player more cunning and more strong than he; and that the Spirit of Evil, though one give him but a hair, will not delay to carry off the whole head. This visible lord of visible nature -- I speak of man -- has, then, wished to create Paradise by chemistry, by fermented drinks; like a maniac who should replace solid furniture and real gardens by decorations painted on canvas and mounted on frames. It is in this degradation of the sense of the Infinite that lies, according to me, the reason of all guilty excesses; from the solitary and concentrated drunkenness of the man of letters, who, obliged to seek in opium an anodyne for a physical suffering, and having thus discovered a well of morbid pleasure, has made of it, little by little, his sole diet, and as it were the sum of his spiritual life; down to the most disgusting sot of the suburbs, who, his head full of flame and of glory, rolls ridiculously in the muck of the roads.

Among the drugs most efficient in creating what I call the artificial ideal, leaving on one side liquors, which rapidly excite gross frenzy and lay flat all spiritual force, and the perfumes, whose excessive use, while rendering more subtle man's imagination, wear out gradually his physical forces; the two most energetic substances, the most convenient and the most handy, are hashish and opium. The analysis of the mysterious effect and the diseased pleasures which these drugs beget, of the inevitable chastisement which results from their prolonged use, and finally the immortality necessarily employed in this pursuit of a false ideal, constitutes the subject of this study.

The subject of opium has been treated already, and in a manner at once so startling, so scientific, and so poetic that I shall not dare to add a word to it. I will therefore content myself in another study, with giving an analysis of this incomparable book, which has never been fully translated into French. The author, an illustrious man of a powerful and exquisite imagination, to-day retired and silent, has dared with tragic candour to write down the delights and the tortures which he once found in opium, and the most dramatic portion of his book is that where he speaks of the superhuman efforts of will which he found it necessary to bring into action in order to escape from the damnation which he had imprudently incurred. To-day I shall only speak of hashish, and I shall speak of it after numerous investigations and minute information; extracts from notes or confidences of intelligent men who had long been addicted to it; only, I shall combine these varied documents into a sort of monograph, choosing a particular soul, and one easy to explain and to define, as a type suitable to experiences of this nature.

CHAPTER II:
WHAT IS HASHISH?

The stories of Marco Polo, which have been so unjustly laughed at, as in the case of some other old travellers, have been verified by men of science, and deserve our belief. I shall not repeat his story of how, after having intoxicated them with hashish (whence the word "assassin") the old Man of the Mountains shut up in a garden filled with delights those of his youngest disciples to whom he wished to give an idea of Paradise as an earnest of the reward, so to speak, of a passive and unreflecting obedience. The reader may consult, concerning the secret Society of Hashishins, the work of Von Hammer-Purgstall, and the note of M. Sylvestre de Sacy contained in vol. 16 of "Mémoires de l'Académie des Inscriptions et Belles-Lettres"; and, with regard to the etymology of the word "assassin," his letter to the editor of *Moniteur* in No. 359 of the year 1809. Herodotus tells us that the Syrians used to gather grains of hemp and throw red-hot stones upon them; so that it was like a vapour-bath, more perfumed than that of any Grecian stove; and the pleasure of it was so acute that it drew cries of joy from them.

Hashish, in effect, comes to us from the East. The exciting properties of hemp were well known in ancient Egypt, and the use of it is very widely spread under different names in India, Algeria, and Arabia Felix; but we have around us, under our eyes, curious examples of the intoxication caused by vegetable emanations. Without speaking of the children who, having played and rolled themselves in heaps of cut lucern, often experience singular attacks of vertigo, it is well known that during the hemp harvest both male and female workers undergo similar effects. One would say that from the harvest rises a miasma which troubles their brains despitefully. The head of the reaper is full of whirlwinds, sometimes laden with reveries; at certain moments the limbs grow weak and refuse their office. We have heard tell of crises of somnambulism as being frequent among the Russian peasants, whose cause, they say, must be attributed to the use of hemp-seed oil in the preparation of food. Who does not know the extravagant behavior of hens which have eaten grains of hemp-seed, and the wild enthusiasm of the horses which the peasants, at weddings and on the feasts of their patron saints, prepare for a steeplechase by a ration of hemp-seed, sometimes sprinkled with wine? Nevertheless, French hemp is unsuitable for preparing hashish, or at least, as repeated experiments have shown, unfitted to give a drug which is equal in power to hashish. Hashish, or Indian hemp (*Cannabis indica*), is a plant of the family *Urticacea*, resembling in every respect the hemp of our latitudes, except that it does not attain the same height. It possesses very extraordinary intoxicating properties, which for some years past have attracted in France the attention of men of science and of the world. It is more or less highly esteemed according to its different sources: that of Bengal is the most prized by Europeans; that, however, of Egypt, of Constantinople, of Persia, and of Algeria enjoys the same properties, but in an inferior degree.

Hashish (or grass; that is to say, the grass par excellence, as if the Arabs had wished to define in a single word the grass source of all material pleasures) has different names, according to its composition and the method of preparation which it has undergone in the country where it has been gathered: in India, bhang; in Africa, teriaki; in Algeria and in Arabia Felix, madjound, &c. It makes considerable difference at what season of the year it is gathered. It possesses its greatest energy when it is in flower. The flowering tops are in consequence the only parts employed in the different preparations of which we are about to speak. The extrait gras of hashish, as the Arabs prepare it, is obtained by boiling the tops of the fresh plant in butter, with a little water. It is strained, after complete evaporation of all humidity, and one thus obtains a preparation which has the appearance of a pomade, in colour greenish yellow, and which possesses a disagreeable odour of hashish and of rancid butter. Under this form it is employed in small pills of two to four grammes in weight, but on account of its objectionable smell, which increases with age, the Arabs conceal the extrait gras in sweetmeats.

The most commonly employed of these sweetmeats, dawamesk, is a mixture of extrait gras, sugar, and various other aromatic substances, such as vanilla, cinnamon, pistachio, almond, musk. Sometimes one even adds a little cantharides, with an object which has nothing in common with the ordinary results of hashish. Under this new form hashish has no disagreeable qualities, and one can take it in a dose of fifteen, twenty, and thirty grammes, either enveloped in a leaf of pain à chanter or in a cup of coffee.

The experiments made by Messrs. Smith, Gastinel, and Decourtive were directed towards the discovery of the active principles of hashish. Despite their efforts, its chemical combination is still little known, but one usually attributes its properties to a resinous matter which is found there in the proportion of about 10 per cent. To obtain this resin the dried plant is reduced to a coarse powder, which is then washed several times with alcohol; this is afterwards partially distilled and evaporated until it reaches the consistency of an extract; this extract is treated with water, which dissolves the gummy foreign matter, and the resin then remains in a pure condition.

This product is soft, of a dark green colour, and possesses to a high degree the characteristic smell of hashish. Five, ten, fifteen centigrammes are sufficient to produce surprising results. But the haschischine, which may be administered under the form of chocolate pastilles or small pills mixed with ginger, has, like the dawamesk and the extrait gras, effects more or less vigorous, and of an extremely varied nature, according to the individual temperament and nervous susceptibility of the hashish-eater; and, more than that, the result varies in the same individual. Sometimes he will experience an immoderate and irresistible gaiety, sometimes a slumber doubtful and thronged with dreams. There are, however, some phenomena which occur regularly enough; above all, in the case of persons of a regular temperament and education; there is a kind of unity in its variety which will allow me to edit, without too much trouble, this monograph on hashish-drunkenness of which I spoke before.

At Constantinople, in Algeria, and even in France, some people smoke hashish mixed with tobacco, but then the phenomena in question only occur under a form much moderated, and, so to say, lazy. I have heard it said that recently, by means of distillation, an essential oil has been drawn from hashish which appears to possess a power much more active than all the preparations hitherto known, but it has not been sufficiently studied for me to speak with certainty of its results. Is it not superfluous to add that tea, coffee, and alcoholic drinks are powerful adjuvants which accelerate more or less the outbreak of this mysterious intoxication?

CHAPTER III:
THE PLAYGROUND OF THE SERAPHIM

What does one experience? What does one see? Marvellous things, is it not so? Wonderful sights? Is it very beautiful? and very terrible? and very dangerous? Such are the usual questions which, with a curiosity mingled with fear, those ignorant of hashish address to its adepts. It is, as it were, the childish impatience to know, resembling that of those people who have never quitted their firesides when they meet a man who returns from distant and unknown countries. They imagine hashish-drunkenness to themselves as a prodigious country, a vast theatre of sleight-of-hand and of juggling, where all is miraculous, all unforseen. -- That is a prejudice, a complete mistake. And since for the ordinary run of readers and of questioners the word "hashish" connotes the idea of a strange and topsy-turvy world, the expectation of prodigious dreams (it would be better to say hallucinations, which are, by the way, less frequent than people suppose), I will at once remark upon the important difference which separates the effects of hashish from the phenomena of dream. In dream, that adventurous voyage which we undertake every night, there is something positively miraculous. It is a miracle whose punctual occurrence has blunted its mystery. The dreams of man are of two classes. Some, full of his ordinary life, of his preoccupations, of his desires, of his vices, combine themselves in a manner more or less bizarre with the objects which he has met in his day's work, which have carelessly fixed themselves upon the vast canvas of his memory. That is the natural dream; it is the man himself. But the other kind of dream, the dream absurd and unforseen, without meaning or connection with the character, the life, and the passions of the sleeper: this dream, which I shall call hieroglyphic, evidently represents the supernatural side of life, and it is exactly because it is absurd that the ancients believed it to be divine. As it is inexplicable by natural causes, they attributed to it a cause external to man, and even to-day, leaving out of account oneiromancers and the fooleries of a philosophical school which sees in dreams of this type sometimes a reproach, sometimes a warning; in short, a symbolic and moral picture begotten in the spirit itself of the sleeper. It is a dictionary which one must study; a language of which sages may obtain the key.

In the intoxication of hashish there is nothing like this. We shall not go outside the class of natural dream. The drunkenness, throughout its duration, it is true, will be nothing but an immense dream, thanks to the intensity of its colours and the rapidity of its conceptions. But it will always keep the idiosyncrasy of the individual. The man has desired to dream; the dream will govern the man. But this dream will be truly the son of its father. The idle man has taxed his ingenuity to introduce artificially the supernatural into his life and into his thought; but, after all, and despite the accidental energy of his experiences, he is nothing but the same man magnified, the same number raised to a very high power. He is brought into subjection, but, unhappily for him, it is not by himself; that is to say, by the part of himself which is already dominant. "He would be angel; he becomes a beast." Momentarily very powerful, if, indeed, one can give the name of power to what is merely excessive sensibility without the control which might moderate or make use of it.

Let it be well understood then, by worldly and ignorant folk, curious of acquaintance with exceptional joys, that they will find in hashish nothing miraculous, absolutely nothing but the natural in a superabundant degree. The brain and the organism upon which hashish operates will only give their ordinary and individual phenomena, magnified, it is true, both in quantity and quality, but always faithful to their origin. Man cannot escape the fatality of his moral and physical temperament. Hashish will be, indeed, for the impressions and familiar thoughts of the man, a mirror which magnifies, yet no more than a mirror.

Here is the drug before your eyes: a little green sweetmeat, about as big as a nut, with a strange smell; so strange that it arouses a certain revulsion, and inclinations to nausea -- as, indeed, any fine and even agreeable scent, exalted to its maximum strength and (so to say) density, would do.

Allow me to remark in passing that this proposition can be inverted, and that the most disgusting and revolting perfume would become perhaps a pleasure to inhale if it were reduced to its minimum quantity and intensity.

There! there is happiness; heaven in a teaspoon; happiness, with all its intoxication, all its folly, all its childishness. You can swallow it without fear; it is not fatal; it will in nowise injure your physical organs. Perhaps (later on) too frequent an employment of the sorcery will diminish the strength of your will; perhaps you will be less a man than you are today; but retribution is so far off, and the nature of the eventual disaster so difficult to define! What is it that you risk? A little nervous fatigue to-morrow -- no more. Do you not every day risk greater punishments for less reward? Very good then; you have even, to make it act more quickly and vigorously, imbibed your dose of extrait gras in a cup of black coffee. You have taken care to have the stomach empty, postponing dinner till nine or ten o'clock, to give full liberty of action to the poison. At the very most you will take a little soup in an hour's time. You are now sufficiently provisioned for a long and strange journey; the steamer has whistled, the sails are trimmed; and you have this curious advantage over ordinary travellers, that you have no idea where you are going. You have made your choice; here's to luck!

I presume that you have taken the precaution to choose carefully your moment for setting out on this adventure. for every perfect debauch demands perfect leisure. You know, moreover, that hashish exaggerates, not only the individual, but also circumstances and environment. You have no duties to fulfil which require punctuality or exactitude; no domestic worries; no lover's sorrows. One must be careful on such points. Such a disappointment, an anxiety, an interior monition of a duty which demands your will and your attention, at some determinate moment, would ring like a funeral bell across your intoxication and poison your pleasure. Anxiety would become anguish, and disappointment torture. But if, having observed all these preliminary conditions, the weather is fine; if your are situated in favourable surroundings, such as a picturesque landscape or a room beautifully decorated; and if in particular you have at command a little music, then all is for the best.

Generally speaking, there are three phases in hashish intoxication, easy enough to distinguish, and it is not uncommon for beginners to obtain only the first symptoms of the first phase. You have heard vague chatter about the marvellous effects of hashish; your imagination has preconceived a special idea, an ideal intoxication, so to say. You long to know if the reality will indeed reach the height of your hope; that alone is sufficient to throw you from the very beginning into an anxious state, favourable enough to the conquering and enveloping tendency of the poison. Most novices, on their first initiation, complain of the slowness of the effects: they wait for them with a puerile impatience, and, the drug not acting quickly enough for their liking, they bluster long rigmaroles of incredulity, which are amusing enough for the old hands who know how hashish acts. The first attacks, like the symptoms of a storm which has held off for a long while, appear and multiply themselves in the bosom of this very incredulity. At first it is a certain hilarity, absurdly irresistible, which possesses you. These accesses of gaiety, without due cause, of which you are almost ashamed, frequently occur and divide the intervals of stupor, during which you seek in vain to pull yourself together. The simplest words, the most trivial ideas, take on a new and strange physiognomy. You are surprised at yourself for having up to now found them so simple. Incongruous likenesses and correspondences, impossible to foresee, interminable puns, comic sketches, spout eternally from your brain. The demon has encompassed you; it is useless to kick against the pricks of this hilarity, as painful as tickling is! From time to time you laugh to yourself at your stupidity and your madness, and your comrades, if you are with others, laugh also, both at your state and their own; but as they laugh without malice, so you are without resentment.

This gaiety, turn by turn idle or acute, this uneasiness in joy, this insecurity, this indecision, last, as a rule, but a very short time. Soon the meanings of ideas become so vague, the conducting thread which binds your conceptions together becomes so tenuous, that none but your accomplices can understand you. And, again, on this subject and from this point of view, no means of verifying it! Perhaps they only think that they understand you, and the illusion is reciprocal. This frivolity, these bursts of laughter, like explosions, seem like a true mania, or at least like the delusion of a maniac, to every man who is not in the same state as yourself. What is more, prudence and good sense, the regularity of the thoughts of him who witnesses, but has been careful not to intoxicate himself, rejoice you and amuse you as if they were a particular form of dementia. The parts are interchanged; his self-possession drives you to the last limits of irony. How monstrous comic is this situation, for a man who is enjoying a gaiety incomprehensible for him who is not placed in the same environment as he! The madman takes pity on the sage, and from that moment the idea of his superiority begins to dawn on the horizon of his intellect. Soon it will grow great and broad, and burst like a meteor.

I was once witness of a scene of this kind which was carried very far, and whose grotesqueness was only intelligible to those who were acquainted, at least by means of observation of others, with the effects of the substance and the enormous difference of diapason which it creates between two intelligences apparently equal. A famous musician, who was ignorant of the properties of hashish, who perhaps had never heard speak of it, finds himself in the midst of a company, several persons of which had taken a portion. They try to make him understand the marvellous effects of it; at these prodigious yarns he smiles courteously, by complaisance, like a man who is willing to play the fool for a minute or two. His contempt is quickly divined by these spirits, sharpened by the poison, and their laughter wounds him; these bursts of joy, this playing with words, these altered countenances -- all this unwholesome atmosphere irritates him, and forces him to exclaim sooner, perhaps, than he would have wished that this is a poor rôle, and that, moreover, it must be very tiring for those who have undertaken it.

The comicality of it lightened them all like a flash; their joy boiled over. "This rôle may be good for you," said he, "but for me, no." "It is good for us; that is all we care about," replies egoistically one of the revellers.

Not knowing whether he is dealing with genuine madmen or only with people who are pretending to be mad, our friend thinks that the part of discretion is to go away; but somebody shuts the door and hides the key. Another, kneeling before him, asks his pardon, in the name of the company, and declares insolently, but with tears, that despite his mental inferiority, which perhaps excites a little pity, they are all filled with a profound friendship for him. He makes up his mind to remain, and even condescends, after pressure, to play a little music.

But the sounds of the violin, spreading themselves through the room like a new contagion, stab -- the word is not too strong -- first one of the revellers, then another. There burst forth deep and raucous sighs, sudden sobs, streams of silent tears. The frightened musician stops, and, approaching him whose ecstasy is noisiest, asks him if he suffers much, and what must be done to relieve him. One of the persons present, a man of common sense, suggests lemonade and acids; but the "sick man," his eyes shining with ecstasy, looks on them both with ineffable contempt. To wish to cure a man "sick" of too much life, "sick" of joy!

As this anecdote shows, goodwill towards men has a sufficiently large place in the feelings excited by hashish: a soft, idle, dumb benevolence which springs from the relaxation of the nerves.

In support of this observation somebody once told me an adventure which had happened to him in this state of intoxication, and as he preserved a very exact memory of his feelings I understood perfectly into what grotesque and inextricable embarrassment this difference of diapason and of pity of which I was just speaking had thrown him. I do not remember if the man in question was at his first or his second experiment; had he taken a dose which was a little too strong, or was it that the hashish had produced, without any apparent cause, effects much more vigorous than the ordinary -- a not infrequent occurrence?

He told me that across the scutcheon of his joy, this supreme delight of feeling oneself full of life and believing oneself full of genius, there had suddenly smitten the bar sinister of terror. At first dazzled by the beauty of his sensations, he had suddenly fallen into fear of them. He had asked himself the question: "What would become of my intelligence and of my bodily organs if this state" (which he took for a supernatural state) "went on By the power of enlargement which the spiritual eye of the patient possesses, this fear must be an unspeakable torment. "I was," he said, "like a runaway horse galloping towards an abyss, wishing to stop and being unable to do so. Indeed, it was a frightful ride, and my thought, slave of circumstance, of milieu, of accident, and of all that may be implied by the word chance, had taken a turn of pure, absolute rhapsody. 'It is too late, it is too late!' I repeated to myself ceaselessly in despair. When this mood, which seemed to me to last for an infinite time, and which I daresay only occupied a few minutes, changed, when I thought that at last I might dive into the ocean of happiness so dear to Easterns which succeeds this furious phase, I was overwhelmed by a new misfortune; a new anxiety, trivial enough, puerile enough, tumbled upon me. I suddenly remembered that I was invited to dinner, to an evening party of respectable people. I foresaw myself in the midst of a well-behaved and discreet crowd, every one master of himself, where I should be obliged to conceal carefully the state of my mind while under the glare of many lamps. I was fairly certain of success, but at the same time my heart almost gave up at the thought of the efforts of will which it would be necessary to bring into line in order to win. By some accident, I know not what, the words of the Gospel, "Woe unto him by whom offences come!" leapt to the surface of my memory, and in the effort to forget them, in concentrating myself upon forgetting them, I repeated them to myself ceaselessly. My catastrophe, for it was indeed a catastrophe, then took a gigantic shape: despite my weakness, I resolved on vigorous action, and went to consult a chemist, for I did not know the antidotes, and I wished to go with a free and careless spirit to the circle where my duty called me; but on the threshold of the shop a sudden thought seized me, haunted me, forced me to reflect. As I passed I had just seen myself in the looking-glass of a shop-front, and my face had startled me. This paleness, these lips compressed, these starting eyes! -- I shall frighten this good fellow, I said to myself, and for what a trifle! Add to that the ridicule which I wished to avoid, the fear of finding people in the shop. But my sudden goodwill towards this unknown apothecary mastered all my other feelings. I imagined to myself this man as being as sensitive as I myself was at this dreadful moment, and as I imagined also that his ear and his soul must, like my own, tremble at the slightest noise, I resolved to go in on tiptoe. 'It would be impossible,' I said to myself, 'to show too much discretion in dealing with a man on whose kindness I am about to intrude.' Then I resolved to deaden the sound of my voice, like the noise of my steps. You know it, this hashish voice: grave, deep, guttural; not unlike that of habitual opium-eaters. The result was the exact contrary of my intention; anxious to reassure the chemist, I frightened him. He was in no way acquainted with this illness; had never even heard of it; yet he looked at me with a curiosity strongly mingled with mistrust. Did he take me for a madman, a criminal, or a beggar? Nor the one nor the other, doubtless, but all these absurd ideas ploughed through my brain. I was obliged to explain to him at length (what weariness!) what the hemp sweetmeat was and what purpose it served, ceaselessly repeating to him that there was no danger, that there was, so far as he was concerned, no reason to be alarmed, and that all that I asked was a method of mitigating or neutralising it, frequently insisting upon the sincere disappointment I felt in troubling him. When I had quite finished (I beg you well to understand all the humiliation which these words contained for me) he asked me simply to go away. Such was the reward of my exaggerated thoughtfulness and goodwill. I went to my evening party; I scandalised nobody. No one guessed the superhuman struggles which I had to make to be like other people; but I shall never forget the tortures of an ultra-poetic intoxication constrained by decorum and antagonised by duty."

Although naturally prone to sympathise with every suffering which is born of the imagination, I could not prevent myself from laughing at this story. The man who told it to me is not cured. He continued to crave at the hands of the cursed confection the excitement which wisdom finds in itself; but as he is a prudent and settled man, a man of the world, he has diminished the doses, which has permitted him to increase their frequency. He will taste later the rotten fruit of his "prudence"!

I return to the regular development of the intoxication. After this first phase of childish gaiety there is, as it were, a momentary relaxation; but new events soon announce themselves by a sensation of coolth at the extremities -- which may even become, in the case of certain persons, a bitter cold -- and a great weakness in all the limbs. You have then "butter fingers"; and in your head, in all your being, you feel an embarrassing stupor and stupefaction. Your eyes start from your head; it is as if they were drawn in every direction by implacable ecstasy. Your face is deluged with paleness; the lips draw themselves in, sucked into the mouth with that movement of breathlessness which characterises the ambition of a man who is the prey of his own great schemes, oppressed by enormous thoughts, or taking a long breath preparatory to a spring. The throat closes itself, so to say; the palate is dried up by a thirst which it would be infinitely sweet to satisfy, if the delights of laziness were not still more agreeable, and in opposition to the least disturbance of the body. Deep but hoarse sighs escape from your breast, as if the old bottle, your body, could not bear the passionate activity of the new wine, your new soul. From one time to another a spasm transfixes you and makes you quiver, like those muscular discharges which at the end of a day's work or on a stormy night precede definitive slumber.

Before going further I should like, à propos of this sensation of coolth of which I spoke above, to tell another story which will serve to show to what point the effects, even the purely physical effects, may vary according to the individual. This time it is a man of letters who speaks, and in some parts of his story one will (I think) be able to find the indications of the literary temperament. "I had taken," he told me, "a moderated dose of extrait gras, and all was going as well as possible. The crisis of gaiety had not lasted long, and I found myself in a state of languor and wonderment which was almost happiness. I looked forward, then, to a quiet and unworried evening: unfortunately chance urged me to go with a friend to the theatre. I took the heroic course, resolved to overcome my immense desire to to be idle and motionless. All the carriages in my district were engaged; I was obliged to walk a long distance amid the discordant noises of the traffic, the stupid conversation of the passers-by, a whole ocean of triviality. My finger-tips were already slightly cool; soon this turned into a most acute cold, as if I had plunged both hands into a bucket of ice-water. But this was not suffering; this needle-sharp sensation stabbed me rather like a pleasure. Yet it seemed to me that this cold enveloped me more and more as the interminable journey went on. I asked two or three times of the person with whom I was if it was actually very cold. He replied to me that, on the contrary, the temperature was more than warm. Installed at last in the room, shut up in the box which had been given me, with three or four hours of repose in front of me, I thought myself arrived at the

Promised Land. The feelings on which I had trampled during the journey with all the little energy at my disposal now burst in, and I give myself up freely to my silent frenzy. The cold ever increased, and yet I saw people lightly clad, and even wiping their foreheads with an air of weariness. This delightful idea took hold of me, that I was a privileged man, to whom alone had been accorded the right to feel cold in summer in the auditorium of a theatre. This cold went on increasing until it became alarming; yet I was before all dominated by my curiosity to know to what degree it could possibly sink. At last it came to such a point, it was so complete, so general, that all my ideas froze, so to speak; I was a piece of thinking ice. I imagined myself as a statue carved in a block of ice, and this mad hallucination made me so proud, excited in me such a feeling of moral well-being, that I despair of defining it to you. What added to my abominable enjoyment was the certainty that all the other people present were ignorant of my nature and of the superiority that I had over them, and then with the pleasure of thinking that my companion never suspected for a moment with what strange feelings I was filled, I clasped the reward of my dissimulation, and my extraordinary pleasure was a veritable secret.

"Besides, I had scarcely entered the box when my eyes had been struck with an impression of darkness which seemed to me to have some relationship with the idea of cold; it is, however, possible that these two ideas had lent each other strength. You know that hashish always invokes magnificences of light, splendours of colour, cascades of liquid gold; all light is sympathetic to it, both that which streams in sheets and that which hangs like spangles to points and roughnesses; the candelabra of salons, the wax candles that people burn in May, the rosy avalanches of sunset. It seems that the miserable chandelier spread a light far too insignificant to quench this insatiable thirst of brilliance. I thought, as I told you, that I was entering a world of shadows, which, moreover, grew gradually thicker, while I dreamt of the Polar night and the eternal winter. As to the stage, it was a stage consecrated to the comic Muse; that alone was luminous; infinitely small and far off, very far, like a landscape seen through the wrong end of a telescope. I will not tell you that I listened to the actors; you know that that is impossible. From time to time my thoughts snapped up on the wing a fragment of a phrase, and like a clever dancing-girl used it as a spring-board to leap into far-distant reveries. You might suppose that a play heard in this manner would lack logic and coherence. Undeceive yourself! I discovered an exceeding subtle sense in the drama created by my distraction. Nothing jarred on me, and I resembled a little that poet who, seeing Esther played for the first time, found it quite natural that Haman should make a declaration of love to the queen. It was, as you guess, the moment where he throws himself at the feet of Esther to beg pardon of his crime. If all plays were listened to on these lines they all, even those of Racine, would gain enormously. The actors seemed to me exceedingly small, and bounded by a precise and clear-cut line, like the figures in Meissonier's pictures. I saw distinctly not only the most minute details of their costumes, their patterns, seams, buttons, and so on, but also the line of separation between the false forehead and the real; the white, the blue, and the red, and all the tricks of make-up; and these Lilliputians were clothed about with a cold and magical clearness, like that which a very clean glass adds to an oil-painting. When at last I was able to emerge from this cavern of frozen shadows, and when, the interior phantasmagoria being dissipated, I came to myself, I experienced a greater degree of weariness than prolonged and difficult work has ever caused me."

It is, in fact, at this period of the intoxication that is manifested a new delicacy, a superior sharpness in each of the senses: smell, sight, hearing, touch join equally in this onward march; the eyes behold the Infinite; the ear perceives almost inaudible sounds in the midst of the most tremendous tumult. It is then that the hallucinations begin; external objects take on wholly and successively most strange appearances; they are deformed and transformed. Then -- the ambiguities, the misunderstandings, and the transpositions of ideas! Sounds cloak themselves with colour; colours blossom into music. That, you will say, is nothing but natural. Every poetic brain in its healthy, normal state, readily conceives these analogies. But I have already warned the reader that there is nothing of the positively supernatural in hashish intoxication; only those analogies possess an unaccustomed liveliness; they penetrate and they envelop; they overwhelm the mind with their masterfulness. Musical notes become numbers; and if your mind is gifted with some mathematical aptitude, the harmony to which you listen, while keeping its voluptuous and sensual character, transforms itself into a vast rhythmical operation, where numbers beget numbers, and whose phases and generation follow with an inexplicable ease and an agility which equals that of the person playing.

It happens sometimes that the sense of personality disappears, and that the objectivity which is the birthright of Pantheist poets develops itself in you so abnormally that the contemplation of exterior objects makes you forget your own existence and confound yourself with them. Your eye fixes itself upon a tree, bent by the wind into an harmonious curve; in some seconds that which in the brain of a poet would only be a very natural comparison becomes in yours a reality. At first you lend to the tree your passions, your desire, or your melancholy; its creakings and oscillations become yours, and soon you are the tree. In the same way with the bird which hovers in the abyss of azure: at first it represents symbolically your own immortal longing to float above things human; but soon you are the bird itself. Suppose, again, you are seated smoking; your attention will rest a little too long upon the bluish clouds which breathe forth from your pipe; the idea of a slow, continuous, eternal evaporation will possess itself of your spirit, and you will soon apply this idea to your own thoughts, to your own apparatus of thought. By a singular ambiguity, by a species of transposition or intellectual barter, you feel yourself evaporating, and you will attribute to your pipe, in which you feel yourself crouched and pressed down like the tobacco, the strange faculty of smoking you!

Luckily, this interminable imagination has only lasted a minute. For a lucid interval, seized with a great effort, has allowed you to look at the clock. But another current of ideas bears you away; it will roll you away for yet another minute in its living whirlwind, and this other minute will be an eternity. For the proportion of time and being are completely disordered by the multitude and intensity of your feelings and ideas. One may say that one lives many times the space of a man's life during a single hour. Are you not, then, like a fantastic novel, but alive instead of being written? There is no longer any equation between the physical organs and their enjoyments; and it is above all on this account that arises the blame which one must give to this dangerous exercise in which liberty is forfeited.

When I speak of hallucinations the word must not be taken in its strictest sense: a very important shade of difference distinguishes pure hallucination, such as doctors have often have occasion to study, from the hallucination, or rather of the misinterpretation of the senses, which arises in the mental state caused by the hashish. In the first case the hallucination is sudden, complete, and fatal; beside which, it finds neither pretext nor excuse in the exterior world. The sick man sees a shape or hears sounds where there are not any. In the second case, where hallucination is progressive, almost willed, and it does not become perfect, it only ripens under the action of imagination. Finally, it has a pretext. A sound will speak, utter distinct articulations; but there was a sound there. The enthusiast eye of the hashish drunkard will see strange forms, but before they were strange and monstrous these forms were simple and natural. The energy, the almost speaking liveliness of hallucination in this form of intoxication in no way invalidates this original difference: the one has root in the situation, and, at the present time, the other has not. Better to explain this boiling over of the imagination, this maturing of the dream, and this poetic childishness to which a hashish-intoxicated brain is condemned, I will tell yet another anecdote. This time it is not an idle young man who speaks, nor a man of letters. It is a woman; a woman no longer in her first youth; curious, with an excitable mind, and who, having yielded to the wish to make acquaintance with the poison, describes thus for another woman the most important of her phases. I transcribe literally.

"However strange and new may be the sensations which I have drawn from my twelve hours' madness -- was it twelve or twenty? in sooth, I cannot tell -- I shall never return to it. The spiritual excitement is too lively, the fatigue which results from it too great; and, to say all in a word, I find in this return to childhood something criminal. Ultimately (after many hesitations) I yielded to curiosity, since it was a folly shared with old friends, where I saw no great harm in lacking a little dignity. But first of all I must tell you that this cursèd hashish is a most treacherous substance. Sometimes one thinks oneself recovered from the intoxication; but it is only a deceitful peace. There are moments of rest, and then recrudescences. Thus, before ten o'clock in the evening I found myself in one of these momentary states; I thought myself escaped from this superabundance of life which had caused me so much enjoyment, it is true, but which was not without anxiety and fear. I sat down to supper with pleasure, like one in that state of irritable fatigue which a long journey produces; for till then, for prudence sake, I had abstained from eating; but even before I rose from the table my delirium had caught me up again as a cat catches a mouse, and the poison began anew to play with my poor brain. Although my house is quite close to that of our friends, and although there was a carriage at my disposal, I felt myself so overwhelmed with the necessity of dreaming, of abandoning myself to this irresistible madness, that I accepted joyfully their offer to keep me till the morning. You know the castle; you know that they have arranged, decorated, and fitted with conveniences in the modern style all that part in which they ordinarily live, but that the part which is usually unoccupied has been left as it was, with its old style and its old adornments. They determined to improvise for me a bedroom in this part of the castle, and for this purpose they chose the smallest room, a kind of boudoir, which, although somewhat faded and decrepit, is none the less charming. I must describe it for you as well as I can, so that you may understand the strange vision which I underwent, a vision which fulfilled me for a whole night, without ever leaving me the leisure to note the flight of the hours.

"This boudoir is very small, very narrow. From the height of the cornice the ceiling arches itself to a vault; the walls are covered with narrow, long mirrors, separated by panels, where landscapes, in the easy style of the decorations, are painted. On the frieze on the four walls various allegorical figures are represented, some in attitudes of repose, others running or flying; above them are brilliant birds and flowers. Behind the figures a trellis rises, painted so as to deceive the eye, and following naturally the curve of the ceiling; this ceiling is gilded. All the interstices between the woodwork and the trellis and the figures are then covered with gold, and at the centre the gold is only interrupted by the geometrical network of the false trellis; you see that that resembles somewhat a very distinguished cage, a very fine cage for a very big bird. I must add that the night was very fine, very clear, and the moon brightly shining; so much so that even after I had put out my candle all this decoration remained visible, not illuminated by my mind's eye, as you might think, but by this lovely night, whose lights clung to all this broidery of gold, of mirrors, and of patchwork colours.

"I was at first much astonished to see great spaces spread themselves out before me, beside me, on all sides. There were limpid rivers, and green meadows admiring their own beauty in calm waters: you may guess here the effect of the panels reflected by the mirrors. In raising my eyes I saw a setting sun, like molten metal that grows cold. It was the gold of the ceiling. But the trellis put in my mind the idea that I was in a kind of cage, or in a house open on all sides upon space, and that I was only separated from all these marvels by the bars of my magnificent prison. In the first place I laughed at the illusion which had hold of me; but the more I looked the more its magic grew great, the more it took life, clearness, and masterful reality. From that moment the idea of being shut up mastered my mind, without, I must admit, too seriously interfering with the varied pleasures which I drew from the spectacle spread around and above me. I thought of myself as of one imprisoned for long, for thousands of years perhaps, in this sumptuous cage, among these fairy pastures, between these marvellous horizons. I imagined myself the Sleeping Beauty; dreamt of an expiation that I must undergo, of deliverance to come. Above my head fluttered brilliant tropical birds, and as my ear caught the sound of the little bells on the necks of the horses which were travelling far away on the main road, the two senses pooling their impressions in a single idea, I attributed to the birds this mysterious brazen chant; I imagined that they sang with a metallic throat. Evidently they were talking to me, and chanting hymns to my captivity. Gambolling monkeys, buffoon-like satyrs, seemed to amuse themselves at this supine prisoner, doomed to immobility; yet all the gods of mythology looked upon me with an enchanting smile, as if to encourage me to bear the sorcery with patience, and all their eyes slid to the corner of their eyelids as if to fix themselves on me. I came to the conclusion that if some faults of the olden time, some sins unknown to myself, had made necessary this temporary punishment, I could yet count upon an overriding goodness, which, while condemning me to a prudent course, would offer me truer pleasures than the dull pleasures which filled our youth. You see that moral considerations were not absent from my dream; but I must admit that the pleasure of contemplating these brilliant forms and colours and of thinking myself the centre of a fantastic drama frequently absorbed all my other thoughts. This stayed long, very long. Did it last till morning? I do not know. All of a sudden I saw the morning sun taking his bath in my room. I experienced a lively astonishment, and despite all the efforts of memory that I have been able to make I have never been able to assure myself whether I had slept or whether I had patiently undergone a delicious insomnia. A moment ago, Night; now, Day. And yet I had lived long; oh, very long! The notion of Time, or rather the standard of Time, being abolished, the whole night was only measurable by the multitude of my thoughts. So long soever as it must have appeared to me from this point of view, it also seemed to me that it had only lasted some seconds; or even that it had not taken place in eternity.

"I do not say anything to you of my fatigue; it was immense. They say that the enthusiasm of poets and creative artists resembles what I experienced, though I have always believed that those persons on whom is laid the task of stirring us must be endowed with a most calm temperament. But if the poetic delirium resembles that which a teaspoonful of hashish confection procured for me I cannot but think that the pleasures of the public cost the poets dear, and it is not without a certain well-being, a prosaic satisfaction, that I at last find myself at home, in my intellectual home; I mean, in real life."

There is a woman, evidently reasonable; but we shall only make use of her story to draw from it some useful notes, which will complete this very compressed summary of the principal feelings which hashish begets.

She speaks of supper as of a pleasure arriving at the right moment; at the moment where a momentary remission, momentary for all its pretence of finality, permitted her to go back to real life. Indeed, there are, as I have said, intermissions, and deceitful calms, and hashish often brings about a voracious hunger, nearly always an excessive thirst. Only, dinner or supper, instead of bringing about a permanent rest, creates this new attack, the vertiginous crisis of which this lady complains, and which was followed by a series of enchanting visions lightly tinged with affright, to which she so assented, resigning herself with the best grace in the world. The tyrannical hunger and thirst of which we speak are not easily assayed without considerable trouble. For the man feels himself so much above material things, or rather he is so much overwhelmed by his drunkenness, that he must develop a lengthy spell of courage to move a bottle or a fork.

The definitive crisis determined by the digestion of food is, in fact, very violent; it is impossible to struggle against it. And such a state would not be supportable if it lasted too long, and if it did not soon give place to another phase of intoxication, which in the case above cited interprets itself by splendid visions, tenderly terrifying, and at the same time full of consolations. This new state is what the Easterns call Kaif. It is no longer the whirlwind or the tempest;

it is a calm and motionless bliss, a glorious resignèdness. Since long you have not been your own master; but you trouble yourself no longer about that. Pain, and the sense of time, have disappeared; or if sometimes they dare to show their heads, it is only as transfigured by the master feeling, and they are then, as compared with their ordinary form, what poetic melancholy is to prosaic grief.

But above all let us remark that in this lady's account (and it is for this purpose that I have transcribed it) it is but a bastard hallucination, and owes its being to the objects of the external world. The spirit is but a mirror where the environment is reflected, strangely transformed. Then, again, we see intruding what I should be glad to call moral hallucination; the patient thinks herself condemned to expiate somewhat; but the feminine temperament, which is ill-fitted to analyse, did not permit her to notice the strangely optimistic character of the aforesaid hallucination. The benevolent look of the gods of Olympus is made poetical by a varnish essentially due to hashish. I will not say that this lady has touched the fringe of remorse, but her thoughts, momentarily turned in the direction of melancholy and regret, have been quickly coloured by hope. This is an observation which we shall again have occasion to verify.

She speaks of the fatigue of the morrow. In fact, this is great. But it does not show itself at once, and when you are obliged to acknowledge its existence you do so not without surprise: for at first, when you are really assured that a new day has arisen on the horizon of your life, you experience an extraordinary sense of well-being; you seem to enjoy a marvellous lightness of spirit. But you are scarcely on your feet when a forgotten fragment of intoxication follows you and pulls you back; it is the badge of your recent slavery. Your enfeebled legs only conduct you with caution, and you fear at every moment to break yourself, as if you were made of porcelain. A wondrous languor -- there are those who pretend that it does not lack charm -- possesses itself of your spirit, and spreads itself across your faculties as a fog spreads itself in a meadow. There, then, you are, for some hours yet, incapable of work, of action, and of energy. It is the punishment of an impious prodigality in which you have squandered your nervous force. You have dispersed your personality to the four winds of heaven -- and now, what trouble to gather it up again and concentrate it!

CHAPTER IV:
THE MAN-GOD

It is time to leave on one side all this jugglery, these big marionettes, born of the smoke of childish brains. Have we not to speak of more serious things -- of modifications of our human opinions, and, in a word, of the morale of hashish?

Up to the present I have only made an abridged monograph on the intoxication; I have confined myself to accentuating its principal characteristics. But what is more important, I think, for the spiritually minded man, is to make acquaintance with the action of the poison upon the spiritual part of man; that is to say, the enlargement, the deformation, and the exaggeration of his habitual sentiments and his moral perception, which present then, in an exceptional atmosphere, a true phenomenon of refraction.

The man who, after abandoning himself for a long time to opium or to hashish, has been able, weak as he has become by the habit of bondage, to find the energy necessary to shake off the chain, appears to me like an escaped prisoner. He inspires me with more admiration than does that prudent man who has never fallen, having always been careful to avoid the temptation. The English, in speaking of opium-eaters, often employ terms which can only appear excessive to those innocent persons who do not understand the horrors of this downfall -- enchained, fettered, enslaved. Chains, in fact, compared to which all others -- chains of duty, chains of lawless love -- are nothing but webs of gauze and spider tissues. Horrible marriage of man with himself! "I had become a bounden slave in the trammels of opium, and my labours and my orders had taken a colouring from my dreams," says the husband of Ligeia. But in how many marvellous passages does Edgar Poe, this incomparable poet, this never-refuted philosopher, whom one must always quote in speaking of the mysterious maladies of the soul, describe the dark and clinging splendours of opium! The lover of the shining Berenice, Egoeus, the metaphysician, speaks of an alteration of his faculties which compels him to give an abnormal and monstrous value to the simplest phenomenon.

"To muse for long unwearied hours, with my attention riveted to some frivolous device on the margin or in the typography of a book; to become absorbed, for the better part of a summer's day, in a quaint shadow falling aslant upon the tapestry or upon the floor; to lose myself, for an entire night, in watching the steady flame of a lamp, or the embers of a fire; to dream away whole days over the perfume of a flower; to repeat monotonously some common word, until the sound, by dint of frequent repetition, ceased to convey any idea whatever to the mind; to lose all sense of motion or physical existence, by means of absolute bodily quiescence long and obstinately persevered in: such were a few of the most common and least pernicious vagaries induced by a condition of the mental faculties, not, indeed, altogether unparalleled, but certainly bidding defiance to anything like analysis or explanation."

And the nervous Augustus Bedloe, who every morning before his walk swallows his dose of opium, tells us that the principal prize which he gains from this daily poisoning is to take in everything, even in the most trivial thing, an exaggerated interest.

"In the meantime the morphine had its customary effect -- that of enduing all the external world with an intensity of interest. In the quivering of a leaf -- in the hue of a blade of grass -- in the shape of a trefoil -- in the humming of a bee -- in the gleaming of a dew-drop -- in the breathing of the wind -- in the faint odours that came from the forest -- there came a whole universe of suggestion -- a gay and motley train of rhapsodical and immethodical thought."

Thus expresses himself, by the mouth of his puppets, the master of the horrible, the prince of mystery. These two characteristics of opium are perfectly applicable to hashish. In the one case, as in the other, the intelligence, formerly free, becomes a slave; but the word rapsodique, which defines so well a train of thought suggested and dictated by the exterior world and the accident of circumstance, is in truth truer and more terrible in the case of hashish. Here the reasoning power is no more than a wave, at the mercy of every current and the train of thought is infinitely more accelerated and more rapsodique; that is to say, clearly enough, I think, that hashish is, in its immediate effect, much more vehement than opium, much more inimical to regular life; in a word, much more upsetting. I do not know if ten years of intoxication by hashish would bring diseases equal to those caused by ten years of opium regimen; I say that, for the moment, and for the morrow, hashish has more fatal results. One is a soft-spoken enchantress; the other, a raging demon.

I wish in this last part to define and to analyse the moral ravage caused by this dangerous and delicious practice; a ravage so great, a danger so profound, that those who return from the fight but lightly wounded appear to me like heroes escaped from the cave of a multiform Proteus, or like Orpheus, conquerors of Hell. You may take, if you will, this form of language for an exaggerated metaphor, but for my part I will affirm that these exciting poisons seem to me not only one of the most terrible and the most sure means which the Spirit of Darkness uses to enlist and enslave wretched humanity, but even one of the most perfect of his avatars.

This time, to shorten my task and make my analysis the clearer, instead of collecting scattered anecdotes I will dress a single puppet in a mass of observation. I must, then, invent a soul to suit my purpose. In his "Confessions" De Quincey rightly states that opium, instead of sending man to sleep, excites him; but only excites him in his natural path, and that therefore to judge of the marvels of opium it would be ridiculous to try it upon a seller of oxen, for such an one will dream of nothing but cattle and grass. Now I am not going to describe the lumbering fancies of a hashish-intoxicated stockbreeder. Who would read them with pleasure, or consent to read them at all? To idealise my subject I must concentrate all its rays into a single circle and polarise them; and the tragic circle where I will gather them together will be, as I have said, a man after my own heart; something analogous to what the eighteenth century called the homme sensible, to what the romantic school named the homme incompris, and to what family folk and the mass of bourgeoisie generally brand with the epithet "original." A constitution half nervous, half bilious, is the most favourable to the evolutions of an intoxication of this kind. Let us add a cultivated mind, exercised in the study of form and colour, a tender heart, wearied by misfortune, but still ready to be made young again; we will go, if you please, so far as to admit past errors, and, as a natural result of these in an easily excitable nature, if not positive remorse, at least regret for time profaned and ill-spent. A taste for metaphysics, an acquaintance with the different hypotheses of philosophy of human destiny, will certainly not be useless conditions; and, further, that love of virtue, of abstract virtue, stoical or mystic, which is set forth in all the books upon which modern childishness feeds as the highest summit to which a chosen soul may attain. If one adds to all that a great refinement of sense -- and if I omitted it it was because I thought it supererogatory -- I think that I have gathered together the general elements which are most common in the modern *homme sensible* of what one might call the lowest common measure of originality. Let us see now what will become of this individuality pushed to its extreme by hashish. Let us follow this progress of the human imagination up to its last and most splendid serai; up to the point of the belief of the individual in his own divinity.

If you are one of these souls your innate love of form and colour will find from the beginning an immense banquet in the first development of your intoxication. Colours will take an unaccustomed energy and smite themselves within your brain with the intensity of triumph. Delicate, mediocre, or even bad as they may be, the paintings upon the ceilings will clothe themselves with a tremendous life. The coarsest papers which cover the walls of inns will open out like magnificent dioramas. Nymphs with dazzling flesh will look at you with great eyes deeper and more limpid than are the sky and sea. Characters of antiquity, draped in their priestly or soldierly costumes, will, by a single glance, exchange with you most solemn confidences. The snakiness of the lines is a definitely intelligible language where you read the sorrowing and the passion of their souls. Nevertheless a mysterious but only temporary state of the mind develops itself; the profoundness of life, hedged by its multiple problems, reveals itself entirely in the sight, however natural and trivial it may be, that one has under one's eyes; the first-come object becomes a speaking symbol. Fourier and Swedenborg, one with his analogies, the other with his correspondences, have incarnated themselves in all things vegetable and animal which fall under your glance, and instead of touching by voice they indoctrinate you by form and colour. The understanding of the allegory takes within you proportions unknown to yourself. We shall note in passing that allegory, that so spiritual type of art, which the clumsiness of its painters has accustomed us to despise, but which is realy one of the most primitive and natural forms of poetry, regains its divine right in the intelligence which is enlightened by intoxication. Then the hashish spreads itself over all life; as it were, the magic varnish. It colours it with solemn hues and lights up all its profundity; jagged landscapes, fugitive horizons, perspectives of towns whitened by the corpse-like lividity of storm or illumined by the gathered ardours of the sunset; abysses of space, allegorical of the abyss of time; the dance, the gesture or the speech of the actors, should you be in a theatre; the first-come phrase if your eyes fall upon a book; in a word, all things; the universality of beings stands up before you with a new glory unsuspected until then. The grammar, the dry grammar itself, becomes something like a book of "barbarous names of evocation." The words rise up again, clothed with flesh and bone; the noun, in its solid majesty; the adjective's transparent robe which clothes and colours it with a shining web; and the verb, archangel of motion which sets swinging the phrase. Music, that other language dear to the idle or the profound souls who seek repose by varying their work, speaks to you of yourself, and recites to you the poem of your life; it incarnates in you, and you swoon away in it. It speaks your passion, not only in a vague, ill-defined manner, as it does in your careless evenings at the opera, but in a substantial and positive manner, each movement of the rhythm marking a movement understood of your soul, each note transforming itself into Word, and the whole poem entering into your brain like a dictionary endowed with life.

It must not be supposed that all these phenomena fall over each other pell-mell in the spirit, with a clamorous accent of reality and the disorder of exterior life; the interior eye transforms all, and gives to all the complement of beauty which it lacks, so that it may be truly worthy to give pleasure. It is also to this essentially voluptuous and sensual phase that one must refer the love of limpid water, running or stagnant, which develops itself so astonishingly in the brain-drunkenness of some artists. The mirror has become a pretext for this reverie, which resembles a spiritual thirst joined to the physical thirst which dries the throat, and of which I have spoken above. The flowing waters, the sportive waters; the musical waterfalls; the blue vastness of the sea; all roll, sing, leap with a charm beyond words. The water opens its arms to you like a true enchantress; and though I do not much believe in the maniacal frenzies caused by hashish, I should not like to assert that the contemplation of some limpid gulf would be altogether without danger for a soul in love with space and crystal, and that the old fable of Undine might not become a tragic reality for the enthusiast.

I think I have spoken enough of the gigantic growth of space and time; two ideas always connected, always woven together, but which at such a time the spirit faces without sadness and without fear. It looks with a certain melancholy delight across deep years, and boldly dives into infinite perspectives. You have thoroughly well understood, I suppose, that this abnormal and tyrannical growth may equally apply to all sentiments and to all ideas. Thus, I have given, I think, a sufficiently fair sample of benevolence. The same is true of love. The idea of beauty must naturally take possession of an enormous space in a spiritual temperament such as I have invented. Harmony, balance of line, fine cadence in movement, appear to the dreamer as necessities, as duties, not only for all beings of creation, but for himself, the dreamer, who finds himself at this period of the crisis endowed with a marvellous aptitude for understanding the immortal and universal rhythm. And if our fanatic lacks personal beauty, do not think he suffers long from the avowal to which he is obliged, or that he regards himself as a discordant note in the world of harmony and beauty improvised by his imagination. The sophisms of hashish are numerous and admirable, tending as a rule to optimism, and one of the principal and the most efficacious is that which transforms desire into realisation. It is the same, doubtless, in many cases of ordinary life; but here with how much more ardour and subtlety! Otherwise, how could a being so well endowed to understand harmony, a sort of priest of the beautiful, how could he make an exception to, and a blot upon, his own theory? Moral beauty and its power, gracefulness and its seduction, eloquence and its achievements, all these ideas soon present themselves to correct that thoughtless ugliness; then they come as consolers, and at last as the most perfect courtiers, sycophants of an imaginary sceptre.

Concerning love, I have heard many persons feel a school-boy curiosity, seeking to gather information from those to whom the use of hashish was familiar, what might not be this intoxication of love, already so powerful in its natural state, when it is enclosed in the other intoxication; a sun within a sun. Such is the question which will occur to that class of minds which I will call intellectual gapers. To reply to a shameful sub-meaning of this part of the question which cannot be openly discussed, I will refer the reader to Pliny, who speaks somewhere of the properties of hemp in such a way as to dissipate any illusions on this subject. One knows, besides, that loss of tone is the most ordinary result of the abuse which men make of their nerves, and of the substances which excite them. Now, as we are not here considering effective power, but motion or susceptibility, I will simply ask the reader to consider that the imagination of a sensitive man intoxicated with hashish is raised to a prodigious degree, as little easy to determine as would be the utmost force possible to the wind in a hurricane, and his senses are subtilised to a point almost equally difficult to define. It is then reasonable to believe that a light caress, the most innocent imaginable, a handshake, for example, may possess a centuple value by the actual state of the soul and of the senses, and may perhaps conduct them, and that very rapidly, to that syncope which is considered by vulgar mortals as the summum of happiness; but it is quite indubitable that hashish awakes in an imagination accustomed to occupy itself with the affections tender remembrances to which pain and unhappiness give even a new lustre. It is no less certain that in these agitations of the mind there is a strong ingredient of sensuality; and, moreover, it may usefully be remarked -- and this will suffice to establish upon this ground the immorality of hashish -- that a sect of Ishmaelites (it is from the Ishmaelites that the Assassins are sprung) allowed its adoration to stray far beyond the Lingam-Yoni; that is to say, to the absolute worship of the Lingam, exclusive of the feminine half of the symbol. There would be nothing unnatural, every man being the symbolic representation of history, in seeing an obscene heresy, a monstrous religion, arise in a mind which has cowardly given itself up to the mercy of a hellish drug and which smiles at the degradation of its own faculties.

Since we have seen manifest itself in hashish intoxication a strange goodwill toward men, applied even to strangers, a species of philanthropy made rather of pity than of love (it is here that the first germ of the Satanic spirit which is to develop later in so extraordinary a manner shows itself), but which goes so far as to fear giving pain to any one, one may guess what may happen to the localised sentimentality applied to a beloved person who plays, or has played, an important part in the moral life of the reveller. Worship, adoration, prayer, dreams of happiness, dart forth and spring up with the ambitious energy and brilliance of a rocket. Like the powder and colouring-matter of the firework, they dazzle and vanish in the darkness. There is no sort of sentimental combination to which the subtle love of a hashish-slave may not lend itself. The desire to protect, a sentiment of ardent and devoted paternity, may mingle themselves with a guilty sensuality which hashish will always know how to excuse and to absolve. It goes further still. I suppose that, past errors having left bitter traces in the soul, a husband or a lover will contemplate with sadness in his normal state a past over-clouded with storm; these bitter fruits may, under hashish, change to sweet fruits. The need of pardon makes the imagination more clever and more supplicatory, and remorse itself, in this devilish drama, which only expresses itself by a long monologue, may act as an incitement and powerfully rekindle the heart's enthusiasm. Yes, remorse. Was I wrong in saying that hashish appeared to a truly philosophical mind as a perfectly Satanic instrument? Remorse, singular ingredient of pleasure, is soon drowned in the delicious contemplation of remorse; in a kind of voluptuous analysis; and this analysis is so rapid that man, this natural devil, to speak as do the followers of Swedenborg, does not see how involuntary it is, and how, from moment to moment, he approaches the perfection of Satan. He admires his remorse, and glorifies himself, even while he is on the way to lose his freedom.

There, then, is my imaginary man, the mind that I have chosen, arrived at that degree of joy and peace where he is compelled to admire himself. Every contradiction wipes itself out; all philosophical problems become clear, or at least appear so; everything is material for pleasure; the plentitude of life which he enjoys inspires him with an unmeasured pride; a voice speaks in him (alas, it is his own!) which says to him: "Thou hast now the right to consider thyself as superior to all men. None knoweth thee, none can understand all that thou thinkest, all that thou feelest; they would, indeed, be incapable of appreciating the passionate love which they inspire in thee. Thou art a king unrecognised by the passers-by; a king who lives, yet none knows that he is king but himself. But what matter to thee? Hast thou not sovereign contempt, which makes the soul so kind?"

We may suppose, however, that from one time to another some biting memory strikes through and corrupts this happiness. A suggestion due to the exterior world may revive a past disagreeable to contemplate. How many foolish or vile actions fill the past! -- actions indeed unworthy of this king of thought, and whose escutcheon they soil? Believe that the hashish-man will bravely confront these reproachful phantoms, and even that he will know how to draw from these hideous memories new elements of pleasure and of pride!

Such will be the evolution of his reasoning. The first sensation of pain being over, he will curiously analyse this action or this sentiment whose memory has troubled his existing glory; the motive which made him act thus; the circumstances by which he was surrounded; and if he does not find in these circumstances sufficient reasons, if not to absolve, at least to extenuate his guilt, do not imagine that he admits defeat. I am present at his reasoning, as at the play of a mechanism seen under a transparent glass. "This ridiculous, cowardly, or vile action, whose memory disturbed me for a moment, is in complete contradiction with my true and real nature, and the very energy with which I condemn it, the inquisitorial care with which I analyse and judge it, prove my lofty and divine aptitude for virtue. How many men could be found in the world of men clever enough to judge themselves; stern enough to condemn themselves?" And not only does he condemn himself, but he glorifies himself; the horrible memory thus absorbed in the contemplation of ideal virtue, ideal charity, ideal genius, he abandons himself frankly to his triumphant spiritual orgy. We have seen that, counterfeiting sacrilegiously the sacrament of penitence, at one and the same time penitent and confessor, he has given himself an easy absolution; or, worse yet, that he has drawn from his contemplation new food for his pride. Now, from the contemplation of his dreams and his schemes of virtue he believes finally in his practical aptitude for virtue; the amorous energy with which he impresses this phantom of virtue seems to him a sufficient and peremptory proof that he possesses the virile energy necessary for the fulfilment of his ideal. He confounds completely dream with action, and his imagination, growing warmer and warmer in face of the enchanting spectacle of his own nature corrected and idealised, substituting this fascinating image of himself for his real personality, so poor in will, so rich in vanity, he ends by declaring his apotheosis in these clear and simple terms, which contain for him a whole world of abominable pleasures: "I am the most virtuous of all men." Does not that remind you a little of Jean-Jacques, who, he also having confessed to the Universe, not without a certain pleasure, dared to break out into the same cry of triumph (or at least the difference is small enough) with the same sincerity and the same conviction? The enthusiasm with which he admired virtue, the nervous emotion which filled his eyes with tears at the sight of a fine action or at the thought of all the fine actions which he would have wished to accomplish, were sufficient to give him a superlative idea of his moral worth. Jean-Jacques had intoxicated himself without the aid of hashish.

Shall I pursue yet further the analysis of this victorious monomania? Shall I explain how, under the dominion of the poison, my man soon makes himself centre of the Universe? how he becomes the living and extravagant expression of the proverb which says that passion refers everything to itself? He believes in his virtue and in his genius; can you not guess the end? All the surrounding objects are so many suggestions which stir in him a world of thought, all more coloured, more living, more subtle than ever, clothed in a magic glamour. "These mighty cities," says he to himself, "where the superb buildings tower one above the other; these beautiful ships balanced by the waters of the roadstead in homesick idleness, that seem to translate our thought 'When shall we set sail for happiness?; these museums full of lovely shapes and intoxicating colours; these libraries where are accumulated the works of science and the dreams of poetry; this concourse of instruments whose music is one; these enchantress women, made yet more charming by the science of adornment and coquetry: all these things have been created for me, for me, for me! For me humanity has toiled; has been martyred, crucified, to serve for pasture, for pabulum to my implacable appetite for emotion, knowledge, and beauty."

I leap to the end, I cut the story short. No one will be surprised that a thought final and supreme jets from the brain of the dreamer: "I am become God."

But a savage and burning cry darts from his breast with such an energy, such a power of production, that if the will and the belief of a drunken man possessed effective power this cry would overthrow the angels scattered in the quarters of the heaven: "I am a god."

But soon this hurricane of pride transforms itself into a weather of calm, silent, reposeful beatitude, and the universality of beings presents itself tinted and illumined by a flaming dawn. If by chance a vague memory slips into the soul of this deplorable thrice-happy one -- "Might there not be another God?" -- believe that he will stand upright before Him; that he will dispute His will, and confront Him without fear.

Who was the French philosopher that, mocking modern German doctrines, said: "I am a god who has dined ill"? This irony would not bite into a spirit uplifted by hashish; he would reply tranquilly: "Maybe I have dined ill; but I am a god."

CHAPTER V:
MORAL

But the morrow; the terrible morrow! All the organs relaxed, tired; the nerves unstretched, the teasing tendency to tears, the impossibility of applying yourself to a continuous task, teach you cruelly that you have been playing a forbidden game. Hideous nature, stripped of its illumination of the previous evening, resembles the melancholy ruins of a festival. The will, the most precious of all faculties, is above all attacked. They say, and it is nearly true, that this substance does not cause any physical ill; or at least no grave one; but can one affirm that a man incapable of action and fit only for dreaming is really in good health, even when every part of him functions perfectly? Now we know human nature sufficiently well to be assured that a man who can with a spoonful of sweetmeat procure for himself incidentally all the treasures of heaven and of earth will never gain the thousandth part of them by working for them. Can you imagine to yourself a State of which all the citizens should be hashish drunkards? What citizens! What warriors! What legislators! Even in the East, where its use is so widely spread, there are Governments which have understood the necessity of proscribing it. In fact it is forbidden to man, under penalty of intellectual decay and death, to upset the primary conditions of his existence, and to break up the equilibrium of his faculties with the surroundings in which they are destined to operate; in a word, to outrun his destiny, to substitute for it a fatality of a new kind. Let us remember Melmoth, that admirable parable. His shocking suffering lies in the disproportion between his marvellous faculties, acquired unostentatiously by a Satanic pact, and the surroundings in which, as a creature of God, he is condemned to live. And none of those whom he wishes to seduce consents to buy from him on the same conditions his terrible privilege. In fact every man who does not accept the conditions of life sells his soul. It is easy to grasp the analogy which exists between the Satanic creations of poets and those living beings who have devoted themselves to stimulants. Man has wished to become God, and soon? -- there he is, in virtue of an inexorable moral law, fallen lower than his natural state! It is a soul which sells itself bit by bit.

Balzac doubtless thought that there is for man no greater shame, no greater suffering, than to abdicate his will. I saw him once in a drawing-room, where they were talking of the prodigious effects of hashish. He listened and asked questions with an amusing attention and vivacity. Those who knew him may guess that it must have interested him, but the idea of thinking despite himself shocked him severely. They offered him dawamesk. He examined it, sniffed at it, and returned it without touching it. The struggle between his almost childish curiosity and his repugnance to submit himself showed strikingly on his expressive face. The love of dignity won the day. Now it is difficult to imagine to oneself the maker of the theory of will, this spiritual twin of Louis Lambert, consenting to lose a grain of this precious substance. Despite the admirable services which ether and chloroform have rendered to humanity, it seems to me that from the point of view of the idealist philosophy the same moral stigma is branded on all modern inventions which tend to diminish human free will and necessary pain. It was not without a certain admiration that I once listened to the paradox of an officer who told me of the cruel operation undergone by a French general at El-Aghouat, and of which, despite chloroform, he died. This general was a very brave man, and even something more: one of those souls to which one naturally applies the term chivalrous. It was not, he said to me, chloroform that he needed, but the eyes of all the army and the music of its bands. That might have saved him. The surgeon did not agree with the officer, but the chaplain would doubtless have admired these sentiments.

It is certainly superfluous, after all thee considerations, to insist upon the moral character of hashish. Let me compare it to suicide, to slow suicide, to a weapon always bleeding, always sharp, and no reasonable person will find anything to object to. Let me compare it to sorcery or to magic, which wishes in working upon matter by means of arcana (of which nothing proves the falsity more than the efficacy) to conquer a dominion forbidden to man or permitted only to him who is deemed worthy of it, and no philosophical mind will blame this comparison. If the Church condemns magic and sorcery it is that they militate against the intentions of God; that they save time and render morality superfluous, and that she -- the Church -- only considers as legitimate and true the treasures gained by assiduous goodwill. The gambler who has found the means to win with certainty we all cheat; how shall we describe the man who tries to buy with a little small change happiness and genius? It is the infallibility itself of the means which constitutes its immorality; as the supposed infallibility of magic brands it with Satanic stigma. Shall I add that hashish, like all solitary pleasures, renders the individual useless to his fellow creatures and society superfluous to the individual, driving him to ceaseless admiration of himself and dragging him day by day towards the luminous abyss in which he admires his Narcissus face? But even if at the price of his dignity, his honesty, and his free will man were able to draw from hashish great spiritual benefits; to make a kind of thinking machine, a fertile instrument? That is a question which I have often heard asked, and I reply to it: In the first place, as I have explained at length, hashish reveals to the individual nothing but himself. It is true that this individual is, so to say, cubed, and pushed to his limit, and as it is equally certain that the memory of impressions survives the orgy, the hope of these utilitarians appears at the first glance not altogether unreasonable. But I will beg them to observe that the thoughts from which they expect to draw so great an advantage are not in reality as beautiful as they appear under their momentary transfiguration, clothed in magic tinsel. They pertain to earth rather than to Heaven, and owe great portion of their beauty to the nervous agitation, to the greediness, with which the mind throws itself upon them. Consequently this hope is a vicious circle. Let us admit for the moment that hashish gives, or at least increases, genius; they forget that it is in the nature of hashish to diminish the will, and that thus it gives with one hand what it withdraws with the other; that is to say, imagination without the faculty of profiting by it. Lastly, one must remember, while supposing a man adroit enough and vigorous enough to avoid this dilemma, that there is another danger, fatal and terrible, which is that of all habits. All such soon transform themselves into necessities. He who has recourse to a poison in order to think will soon be unable to think without the poison. Imagine to yourself the frightful lot of a man whose paralysed imagination will no longer function without the aid of hashish or of opium! In philosophical states the human mind, to imitate the course of the stars, is obliged to follow a curve which loops it back to its point of departure, when the circle must ultimately close. At the beginning I spoke of this marvellous state into which the spirit of man sometimes finds itself thrown as if by a special favour. I have said that, ceaselessly aspiring to rekindle his hopes and raise himself towards the infinite, he showed (in every country and in every time) a frenzied appetite for every substance, even those which are dangerous, which, by exalting his personality, are able to bring in an instant before his eyes this bargain Paradise, object of all his desires; and at last that this daring spirit, driving without knowing it his chariot through the gates of Hell, by this very fact bore witness to his original greatness. But man is not so God-forsaken, so barren of straightforward means of reaching Heaven, that he need invoke pharmacy and witchcraft. He has no need to sell his soul to buy intoxicating caresses and the friendship of the Hur Al'ain. What is a Paradise which must be bought at the price of eternal salvation? I imagine a man (shall I say a Brahmin, a poet, or a Christian philosopher?) seated upon the steep Olympus of spirituality; around him the Muses of Raphael or of Mategna, to console him for his long fasts and his assiduous prayers, weave the noblest dances, gaze on him with their softest glances and their most dazzling smiles; the divine Apollo, master of all knowledge (that of Francavilla, of Albert Dürer, of Goltzius, or another -- what does it matter? Is there not an Apollo for every man who deserves one?), caresses with his bow his most sensitive strings; below him, at the foot of the mountain, in the brambles and the mud, the human fracas; the Helot band imitates the grimaces of enjoyment and utters howls which the sting of the poison tears from its breast; and the poet, saddened, says to himself: "These unfortunate ones, who have neither fasted nor prayed, who have refused redemption by the means of toil, have asked of black magic the means to raise themselves at a single blow to transcendental life. Their magic dupes them, kindles for them a false happiness, a false light; while as for us poets and philosophers, we have begotten again our soul upon ourselves by continuous toil and contemplation; by the unwearied exercise of will and the unfaltering nobility of aspiration we have created for ourselves a garden of Truth, which is Beauty; of Beauty which is Truth. Confident in the word which says that faith removeth mountains, we have accomplished the only miracle which God has licensed us to perform."

www.ingramcontent.com/pod-product-compliance
Lightning Source LLC
LaVergne TN
LVHW041500070426
835507LV00009B/712